BACKYARD WILDLIFE

Armadillos

by Kari Schuetz

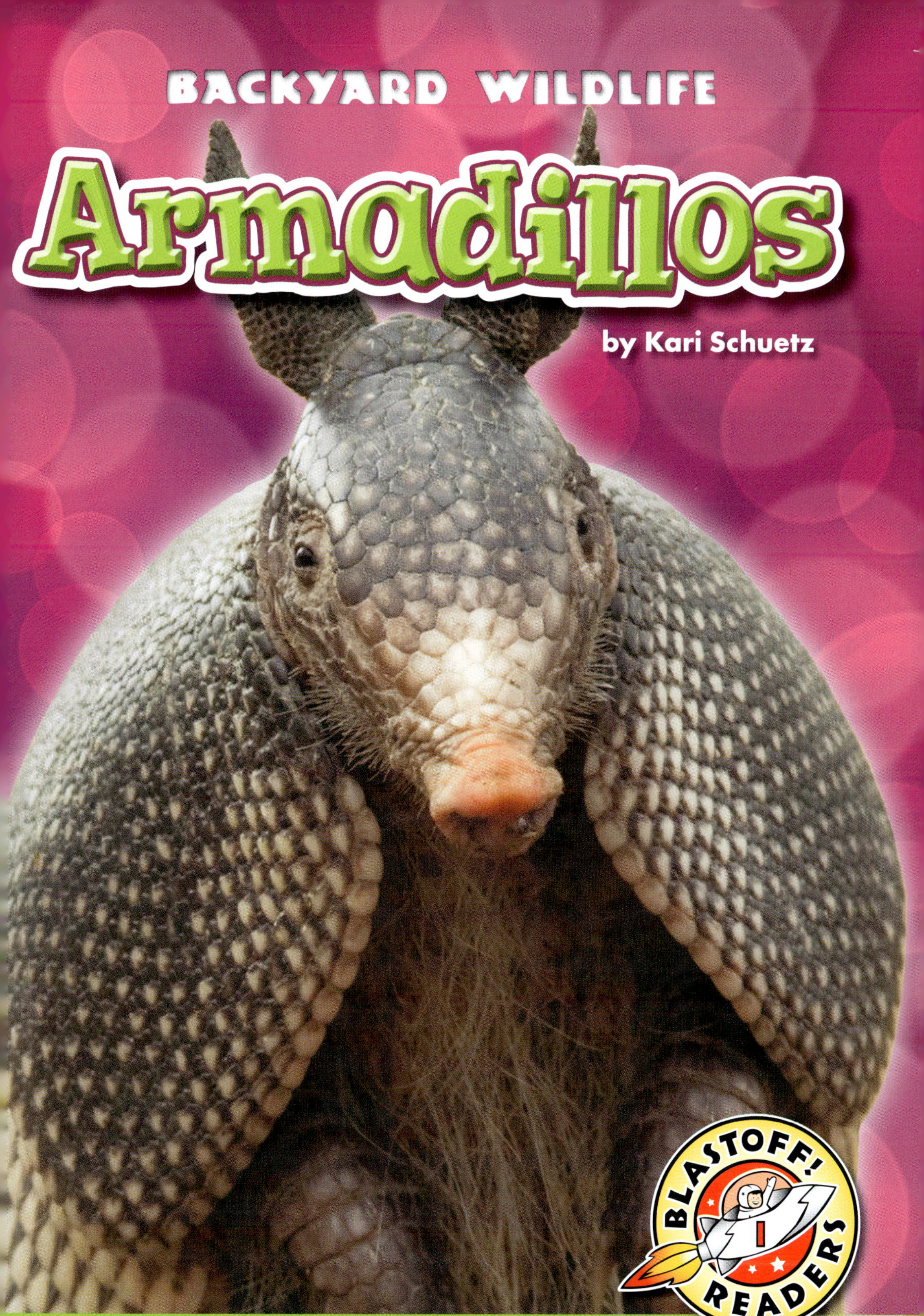

BLASTOFF! READERS 1

BELLWETHER MEDIA • MINNEAPOLIS, MN

Note to Librarians, Teachers, and Parents:

Blastoff! Readers are carefully developed by literacy experts and combine standards-based content with developmentally appropriate text.

Level 1 provides the most support through repetition of high-frequency words, light text, predictable sentence patterns, and strong visual support.

Level 2 offers early readers a bit more challenge through varied simple sentences, increased text load, and less repetition of high-frequency words.

Level 3 advances early-fluent readers toward fluency through increased text and concept load, less reliance on visuals, longer sentences, and more literary language.

Level 4 builds reading stamina by providing more text per page, increased use of punctuation, greater variation in sentence patterns, and increasingly challenging vocabulary.

Level 5 encourages children to move from "learning to read" to "reading to learn" by providing even more text, varied writing styles, and less familiar topics.

Whichever book is right for your reader, Blastoff! Readers are the perfect books to build confidence and encourage a love of reading that will last a lifetime!

This edition first published in 2012 by Bellwether Media, Inc.

Library of Congress Cataloging-in-Publication Data
Schuetz, Kari.
Armadillos / by Kari Schuetz.
p. cm. – (Blastoff! Readers: Backyard wildlife)
Includes bibliographical references and index.
Summary: "Developed by literacy experts for students in kindergarten through grade three, this book introduces armadillos to young readers through leveled text and related photos"–Provided by publisher.
ISBN 978-1-60014-594-0 (hardcover : alk. paper)
1. Armadillos–Juvenile literature. I. Title.
QL737.E23S38 2012
599.3'12–dc22 2011002234

Printed in the United States of America, North Mankato, MN.

080111 1187

Contents

Armadillos are animals with long, pointed **snouts**.

snout

They have hard shells on their backs. Skin and hair cover their bellies.

Armadillos make homes in grasslands and forests. They live in logs or **burrows**.

They dig burrows with their strong legs and sharp **claws**.

claws

Armadillos sink in water. They can hold their breath for six minutes.

They can also fill their bellies with air. This lets them float in water.

Armadillos eat ants, termites, and other **insects**. They use their long, sticky tongues to grab food.

Armadillos run from coyotes, bears, and other **predators**. Their shells protect them while they run.

Armadillos can jump up to 4 feet (1.2 meters) in the air when scared. Up, up and away!

Glossary

burrows–holes in the ground that some animals dig; armadillos live in burrows.

claws–sharp, curved nails on the toes of some animals; armadillos use their claws to dig.

insects–small animals with six legs and hard outer bodies; insect bodies are divided into three parts.

predators–animals that hunt other animals for food

snouts–the noses and jaws of some animals

To Learn More

AT THE LIBRARY

Jango-Cohen, Judith. *Let's Look at Armadillos.* Minneapolis, Minn.: Lerner Publications, 2011.

McKerley, Jennifer Guess. *Amazing Armadillos.* New York, N.Y.: Random House, 2009.

Swinburne, Stephen R. *Armadillo Trail: The Northward Journey of the Armadillo.* Honesdale, Pa.: Boyds Mills Press, 2009.

ON THE WEB

Learning more about armadillos is as easy as 1, 2, 3.

1. Go to www.factsurfer.com.
2. Enter "armadillos" into the search box.
3. Click the "Surf" button and you will see a list of related Web sites.

With factsurfer.com, finding more information is just a click away.

Index

The images in this book are reproduced through the courtesy of: Bill Draker/Photolibrary, front cover, p. 7; Minden Pictures/Masterfile, pp. 5, 9; Juan Martinez, pp. 9 (left), 11 (small), 17 (left, middle), 19 (right), 21; Andrey Tiyk, p. 9 (right); Morales Morales/Photolibrary, pp. 11, 19; Heidi & Hans-Juergen Koch/Minden Pictures, pp. 13, 17; Claus Meyer/Minden Pictures, p. 15; Joseph Calev, p. 17 (right); Bobby Deal/RealDealPhoto, p. 19 (right).